In the *Shadow* of the

Cross

A study of the characters who met at the crucifixion

6 GROUP BIBLE STUDIES FOR LENT

TREVOR J. PARTRIDGE

Concept development, editing, design and production by CWR.
Photographs: Roger Walker
Printed by Spain by Espace Grafic
ISBN: 1-85345-247-5

Contents

Introduction

Why is this Lent Study Different?

Lent is a time of hope, aspiration and new life. The expectation of a new dawn and the promise of resurrection life for all. A time of journeying with Jesus as He makes His way towards Jerusalem and ultimately to Calvary. He did not journey alone, others were with Him, some close at hand, some watching from afar. Many Lent studies focus on specific points in the story of Jesus, but ours will focus on the people who eventually stood in the shadow of His cross.

Some would follow Him all the way to Golgotha's hill and would be able to say, 'I was there when they nailed Him to the tree.' They were eyewitnesses – some willing participants, some bystanders, others helpless observers and some had no choice. Who were they? Why were they there? What led them to the foot of the cross and what was their response at the end of that day? Let me ask you a question, in the words of the old Negro spiritual, 'Were *you* there when they crucified my Lord, were *you* there?'

In the Shadow of the Cross

There are two well-known pictures with the same title, 'The shadow of the cross'. One, by Holman Hunt, represents the interior of a carpenter's workshop, with Joseph and the Boy Jesus at work. Mary is also present. The Boy Jesus pauses in His work and, as He stretches Himself, the shadow of a cross is formed on the wall. The other picture is a popular engraving that depicts the Infant Jesus running with outstretched arms to His mother. As He runs towards her the shadow of the cross is formed.

Although both these pictures are fanciful in their portrayal, the underlying intent and idea depicting the certainty of the cross for the Christ child is assuredly right. All His life He lived in the shadow of Calvary.

There is no question that the death of Jesus was in view almost from the earliest days of His life. Mary, His mother, who would be one of those gathering at the foot of the cross in those awful final moments of agonising death a mother hopes she never has to witness, had an early hint when the aged Simeon, who rejoiced with her at Jesus' birth, said to her, 'And a sword will pierce your own soul too' (Luke 2:35).

The moment would come when Jesus would reveal the shadow of the cross to His disciples. The first hints seemed vague and fragmentary, but as the days progressed, the fact and its purpose became clearer and clearer. 'Destroy this temple, and I will raise it again in three days' (John 2:19), Jesus had proclaimed at the outset of His ministry, and to the seeking Nicodemus, 'The Son of Man must be lifted up' (John 3:14).

Although He told His disciples beforehand what lay ahead of Him, it was a long time before the realisation dawned upon their souls, that they were also living in the shadow of His cross. To them the cross was a strange and alien idea, some barbaric form of execution inflicted upon the Jews by the Romans as a severe form of punishment and retribution. The sense of its eternal magnitude eluded them and they avoided the thought of its remotest possibility for a long time.

The defining moment dawned at Caesarea Philippi when, in response to Jesus' question, 'Who do you say I am?' Peter affirms with the words, 'You are the Christ, the Son of the living God' (Matt. 16:15–16). Jesus knew that the time had come to entrust His disciples with the revelation of the full import of the shadow of the cross. Although it had been implicit, it was now time to open their minds fully to a truth that to them would seem so blindingly new and unbelievably shocking. 'From that time on, Jesus began to explain to his disciples that he must go to Jerusalem and suffer many things at the hands of the elders, chief priests and teachers of the law, and that he must be killed and on the third day raised to life' (Matt. 16:21). As He tells these men what He had so surely known from His early years, that He will die at Jerusalem and those who have opposed Him will win out, the immediate response is one of consternation and disbelief. It was so shocking and indecent a proposal that Peter, always the first to speak up, openly rebukes Him and rebuts the very thought and possibility as his sense of love and devotion rises in indignation. Blustering and posturing he protests, 'This shall never happen to you!' (Matt. 16:22).

Jesus, knowing Simon Peter would have Him go some other way of earthly greatness rather than the ignominy and shame of the cross to usher in the kingdom, and not willing to be deflected or compromised, sees this foolish notion for what it is. He rebukes Satan's attempts to divert Him from the shadow of the cross and invites His disciples to also take up their cross and follow Him all the way to Calvary.

As the day dawns on Golgotha's hill on that tumultuous and solemn morning, the gathering crowd assemble as Christ becomes the central figure of the unfolding drama.

Suggestions for Group Leaders

This group study is designed for use during Lent. Group Leaders need to encourage Group Members to read various elements – Opening and Closing Prayers, the Eye Opener, the Icebreaker, the Bible Readings and the Characters Seen at Calvary sessions. In this way they can participate in the whole study, and often the change of voice and pace helps them to concentrate better.

The Leader should facilitate the Discussion Starters section – having first read the relevant Leader's Notes, and lead the Final Thoughts section.

Suggestions for Group Members

Discussion groups are most effective and enjoyable when all members participate in an atmosphere of encouragement and respect. Be on time and treat other group members as you would like them to treat you. Listen attentively, be encouraging and be prepared to volunteer to read one of the different sections of the study. Be careful not to take more than your share of the group's time. Give others the opportunity to speak. Pray that you will be open to what God will teach you through the study and through other group members. If you need individual prayer, or to share a personal problem, do so privately with your leader after the meeting has ended. If possible, let your leader know of your need ahead of time.

Suggestions on Using This Book

Each study is designed to last a minimum of one hour, a maximum of one and half hours, and is divided into different sections. Make use of every section, as they are designed to lead you through the study in a helpful, progressive way.

Each study contains:
- Opening Prayer
- Eye Opener
- Icebreaker
- Bible Reading
- The Characters Seen at Calvary
- Discussion Starters
- Final Thoughts
- Closing Prayer
- For Further Study

Opening Prayers (1 to 2 minutes)

Suggested opening short prayers are given for each study to enable those who may not be used to praying in a small group setting to feel comfortable and to concentrate on the words. Those leading prayers may also use their own prayers.

Eye Openers (3 minutes)

These are designed to set the scene for the study and to arouse initial interest.

Icebreakers (10 minutes maximum)

Icebreakers are designed to encourage group members to share their thoughts and experiences with one another in a non-threatening way. These are mainly simple exercises to ease any initial unfamiliarity with each other and to promote conversation and participation before the main study.

Bible Readings (5 minutes)

Some who may feel uncomfortable leading Prayers, Eye Openers or Icebreakers may prefer to participate by reading a Bible passage.

The Characters Seen at Calvary (10 minutes)

This section should be read out by one person so that everyone can follow the text.

Discussion Starters (45 minutes maximum)

These are designed to stimulate group discussion and to encourage members to apply the teaching from the study to their own lives.

Encourage discussion that goes beyond the suggested questions, providing you do not stray too far from the subject. Leaders need to keep the group on track, to ensure that all the discussion starters are covered.

Final Thoughts (2 minutes)

The leader should read this section to focus the group's thoughts on the truths expressed in the study.

Closing Prayer (1 to 2 minutes)
Suggestions are given for short closing prayers to draw the study to a definite close. Personal prayers can also be added.

For Further Study
These are suggestions for further study of other relevant Bible passages to use after the group meeting.

Leader's Notes
There is a section of Leader's Notes for each of the six studies at the end of this book. It is suggested that the group leader read the relevant section in preparation before each study.

For Further Reading
Captivated by Christ, Wesley W. Nelson
The Jesus of History, T.R. Glover
Jesus of Galilee, F. Warburton Lewis
They Met at Calvary, W.E. Sangster
The Power of the Cross, Steve Green
The Day Christ Died, Jim Bishop
Jesus in His Time, Daniel Rops
More than a Carpenter, Josh McDowell

The Pharisees and Priests
Self-righteous Scholars

Opening Prayer

Lord, it is so easy to get caught up in dogma and creed and miss You at the centre of it. As we consider today those who stood in the shadow of the cross with only a religious framework to their lives, help us not to be blinded by bigotry and pride as they were. So often, Lord, we are unable and unwilling to break out of our own narrow mind-set, routines and formalities that push You to the margins, having a form of godliness yet unable to embrace You and Your Truth more fully. Father, let the shadow of the cross continue to fall over our lives in more meaningful ways. Amen

Eye Opener

In the time of Christ, if you met a man in the streets of Jerusalem dressed in a long robe with broad borders, blue fringes, tassels, with a small black box strapped to his forehead and left arm and walking with his eyes half shut or face upturned to the sky, you could be sure he was a Pharisee.

Watching him, you would see him step out of the way of a group of noisy children, or turn his head aside when a woman passed with her water pot. You would see him draw his robe closer to himself when he saw a tax collector, in case even the fringe of his cloak touched him. You would see a deeply religious man following a code of strict rules, the Law, believing that no one could be good unless they kept it. 'Pharisee' meant 'one who is different from others and separated from them'.

The Sadducees were different again in that they came directly from the priestly line. You could only be born a Sadducee. Their influence was not so much religious as political. Their lineage was exclusive and no one could be born into the higher order of priests who did not belong to a certain family tree. Politics and religion had become intertwined and priests were not only spiritual leaders but politicians too, who could wield great power and authority.

Icebreaker
Jesus told a story in Luke, of a Pharisee and a publican. From memory, get the group to retell the story with each person adding whatever they can remember from it.

Bible Readings
Matthew 23:1–3, 23–28, *The Message*
Now Jesus turned to address His disciples, along with the crowd that had gathered with them. 'The religion scholars and Pharisees are competent teachers in God's Law. You won't go wrong in following their teachings on Moses. But be careful about following *them*. They talk a good line, but they don't live it. They don't take it into their hearts and live it out in their behavior. It's all spit-and-polish veneer ...

'You're hopeless, you religion scholars and Pharisees! Frauds! You keep meticulous account books, tithing on every nickel and dime you get, but on the meat of God's Law, things like fairness and compassion and commitment – the absolute basics! – you carelessly take it or leave it. Careful bookkeeping is commendable, but the basics are required. Do you have any idea how silly you look, writing a life story that's wrong from start to finish, nitpicking over commas and semicolons?

'You're hopeless, you religion scholars and Pharisees! Frauds! You burnish the surface of your cups and bowls so they sparkle in the sun, while the insides are maggoty with your greed and gluttony. Stupid Pharisee! Scour the insides, and then the gleaming surface will mean something.

'You're hopeless, you religion scholars and Pharisees! Frauds! You're like manicured grave plots, grass clipped and the flowers bright, but six feet down it's all rotting bones and worm-eaten flesh. People look at you and think you're saints, but beneath the skin you're total frauds.'

Matthew 27:41–43, *The Message*
The high priests, along with the religion scholars and leaders, were right there mixing it up with the rest of them, having a great time poking fun at him: 'He saved others – he can't save

himself! King of Israel, is he? Then let him get down from that cross. We'll *all* become believers then!'

The Sanctimonious Self-righteous

On His journey from Nazareth to Calvary, Jesus had encountered a group of men who would now play a major part in His death and crucifixion. Although they had not realised it, the shadow of the cross was cast over them. Now they stood directly in the reality of its dark image on this awesome day. They were the self-satisfied, smug, complacent religious leaders of the day. The Pharisees, the Sadducees, the teachers of the law, who had become particularly hostile and antagonistic towards Him.

Standing in the shadow of the cross, the very scene exposed their self-righteous hypocrisy as they looked on at the wicked deed they had initiated. Would shame and regret grip their consciences as Christ's searing words must have echoed in their hearts? Would they finally admit that their righteousness was as filthy rags, turn from their pious, sanctimonious superiority and surrender to the Saviour? No, to the last they were spitting out their self-righteous venom at the Lord Jesus, mocking and reviling Him as an impostor, along with the rest of the crowd.

He had grown too popular, the people were following after Him in droves, multitudes were flocking to see and hear Him. The reports of His impact were growing by the day, amazing stories were circulating and while the Pharisees and Sadducees didn't believe them for a moment, the people did and that angered and troubled them deeply. The Sadducees feared a political uprising and questioned His political intentions. The Pharisees feared that the exposure of their hypocritical façade would undermine and destroy their credibility and influence. The Pharisees and Sadducees colluded together to put Him to death on a Roman cross.

To maintain his self-righteous position and moral standing, the Pharisee was governed by rules and rituals, quite often about small and insignificant things. For instance, when it came to meals there was a rule about how he washed his hands, how he cooked and ate his food, and washed the dishes. He would meticulously follow rules for fasting and prayer, rules about the Sabbath, rules about this, that and the other. So much time was spent concentrating on the minutiae of the rules that he forgot to be loving, kind, considerate, unselfish or to offer help and support to the poor and needy.

At the street corner, or the market place he would make a great pietistic display and begin to pray – a great many long prayers in order to let others know how righteous and holy he was. He was full of pride and religious arrogance.

You can imagine their consternation when on many occasions Jesus exposed the Pharisees for what they were. 'You hypocrites!' He boomed out, much to the delight of the common onlooker. 'Woe to you ... You snakes! You brood of vipers! How will you escape being condemned to hell?' (Matt. 23:33). Popular with the common folk, He definitely was not popular with the Pharisees.

The Sadducees were aristocratic Jews, exercising the highest office of priesthood. When the Roman Empire invaded and eventually incorporated Palestine, the Sadducees and the Romans formed its political alliance. The Sadducees therefore became the pawns and puppets of Rome, headed by the high priests, Caiaphas and Annas (Luke 3:2). Politics prevailed over spirituality as they sought to accommodate Rome and please their political masters. Compromise and convenience became the order of the day, as they went about their self-seeking task of ruling and controlling the people.

When Jesus burst onto the scene, He challenged the status quo. He disturbed the face of religious respectability, threatening the stability of their cosy political arrangements. He was gaining a reputation and gathering a following that was now a challenge to the priestly aristocracy and the religious bigotry of the day. In the eyes of the Pharisees and Sadducees, there was a dangerous

impostor abroad, a provincial Galilean preacher man, a fanatical hot gospeller from the north, a blasphemous hothead claiming to be the Son of God who was winning the hearts and minds of the people. They resented His popularity and were angered by His authority. He was a dangerous threat to them and had to be stopped at all costs.

They had schemed and conspired, plotted and connived, then taken counsel with the Sanhedrin, on a trumped-up charge of blasphemy, to put Him to death by delivering Him into the hands of Pontius Pilate, to face trial and execution.

Now, as they stood in the direct, dim shadow of the cross, unwilling to admit their own self-righteousness, stubbornness and sinfulness, they profanely vilified Him as a deceiver and an impostor. 'He saved others,' they taunted, 'but he cannot save himself.' No ranting taunts, reviling jibes or heinous insults from so-called religious leaders, as demeaning, humiliating and painful as they were, would distract or divert Him now.

As P.P. Bliss the hymn writer put it:

Bearing shame and scoffing rude
in my place condemned He stood.

'He's the King of Israel,' they continued to mock. 'Let him come down now from the cross.' But the matter was settled, the shadow of the cross led to the cross itself. No cross – no Christ – no crown.

As another hymn writer, Katherine Kelly, put it:

Was it the nails, O Saviour, that bound thee to the tree?
Nay, 'twas Thine everlasting love,
Thy love for me, for me.

He did not need to come down from the cross simply at their behest to prove Himself the Christ. No, He emptied Himself of righteousness, taking into Himself the sin and unrighteousness of a lost world. The miracle of Calvary was not the need to prove Himself to satisfy some self-righteous, unbelieving, religious bigots, but His coming up from the grave in full and flowing resurrection life to redeem lost sinners. Through His death and resurrection the provision of a robe of righteousness was made available for all those willing to admit that their own righteousness is as filthy rags and who are willing to make the exchange. It was purchased for them with His own blood shed upon the cross at the hands of cruel men. What an opportunity missed by these men in the shadow of the cross to make that exquisite exchange.

Discussion Starters

1. Highlight and discuss the core issue with which Jesus confronted the Pharisees.

_____

_____

_____

_____

2. Discuss the difference between religious bigotry and principled convictions.

_____

_____

_____

_____

3. Who would you liken the Pharisees to in our modern day?

_____

_____

_____

_____

4. What are some of the issues that made these groups antagonistic to Christ?

_____

_____

_____

_____

5. Think back to some of your own antagonisms to Christ prior to your conversion, and share.

_____

_____

_____

_____

6. What are some of the Pharisaic attitudes we often find in our own hearts?

_____

_____

_____

_____

7. How would you define self-righteousness, and how does it manifest itself?

_____

_____

_____

_____

8. What can an overwhelming sense of pride drive us to do?

_____

_____

_____

_____

Final Thoughts

The thing that drove these men was an overwhelming, overriding self-righteousness mixed with fear. Normally they had little to do with each other. Pharisees were puritans, Sadducees were not. Pharisees passionately moral, Sadducees only mildly so. The Pharisees' passion was religion, the Sadducees' politics. Pharisees were in close touch with the people, Sadducees remote from them. Pharisees believed in resurrection, Sadducees denied it. There were so many differences that they were continually at loggerheads. The roads they travelled to the cross were diverse and different, yet they converged together to protect their own self-righteous positions, causing the unholy alliance that perpetrated the greatest crime ever recorded in human history.

Closing Prayer

Oh God, when I see the depths and lengths that the human heart will go to in its pride and fear, I am so grateful that You paid the price on the cross to deal a death blow to all my self-righteous ambitions and religious façade. I come to You afresh today recognising that any and all the righteousness that I can muster up through my good works and pious activity is insufficient. Clothe me afresh today I pray with Your spotless robe of righteousness, enabling me to be loving, kind, considerate and unselfish. Amen

For Further Study

Matthew 6:1–4; Mark 11:15–18; Luke18:9–14; Acts 23:1–11; James 1:26

The Common People
Callous Crowd

Opening Prayer

Lord, how good it is to withdraw from the crowd mentality at this time of Lent and focus on Your redemptive work at the cross. I thank You that You treat and accept each of us as individuals, that we are not lost in the faceless crowd, but are objects of Your love and grace. Often, Lord, it is hard to withstand the pressures, demands and pull of those around us. Give us courage to be willing to stand up for what we know to be right, against the popular view of the crowd, and the strength not to be carried along by their opinions and values.

Eye Opener

The crowd cried out, 'Let his blood be on us and on our children' (Matt 27:25). In less than 40 years their city and temple were overthrown and destroyed. More than a million people perished in the siege. Thousands died by famine; thousands by disease; thousands by the sword; and their blood ran down the streets like water, so that, Josephus the historian says, it extinguished things that were burning in the city. Thousands were crucified, suffering the same punishment that they had inflicted on the Messiah. So great was the number of those who were crucified that, Josephus says, they were obliged to cease from it, 'room being wanting for the crosses, and crosses for the men'. Truly it is an awesome thing to fall into the hands of the living God.

Icebreaker

You have just received a note from an old friend. 'Thank God. I've just won the rollover jackpot and need never work again. Liberation! What more could a person ask for, everyone does the lotto and I've been the lucky one. Be happy for me. The £20 I owe you is in the post plus a little extra as a thank you, with your invitation to the celebration party next month.'

Break down into threes and discuss how you would respond and why.

Bible Reading
Matthew 27:15–26, *The Message*

It was an old custom during the Feast for the governor to pardon a single prisoner named by the crowd. At the time, they had the infamous Jesus Barabbas in prison. With the crowd before him, Pilate asked, 'Which prisoner do you want me to pardon: Jesus Barabbas, or Jesus the so-called Christ?' He knew it was through sheer spite that they had turned Jesus over to him.

While court was still in session, Pilate's wife sent him a message: 'Don't get mixed up in judging this noble man. I've just been through a long and troubled night because of a dream about him.'

Meanwhile, the high priests and religious leaders had talked the crowd into asking for the pardon of Barabbas and the execution of Jesus.

The governor asked, 'Which of the two do you want me to pardon?'

They said, 'Barabbas!'

'Then what do I do with Jesus, the so-called Christ?'

They all shouted, 'Nail him to a cross!'

He objected, 'But for what crime?'

But they yelled all the louder, 'Nail him to a cross!'

When Pilate saw that he was getting nowhere and that a riot was imminent, he took a basin of water and washed his hands in full sight of the crowd, saying, 'I'm washing my hands of responsibility for this man's death. From now on, it's in your hands. You're judge and jury.'

The crowd answered, 'We'll take the blame, we and our children after us.'

Then he pardoned Barabbas. But he had Jesus whipped, and then handed over for crucifixion.

The Callous Crowd

Wherever Christ went, people followed. The fact is that crowds were constantly drawn to Him. At His baptism on the banks of the Jordan, to hear Him give the Sermon on the Mount, for the feeding of the 5,000, at the house in Capernaum, and on many

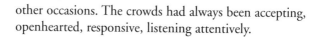

other occasions. The crowds had always been accepting, openhearted, responsive, listening attentively.

Was this the same crowd who now stood in the shadow of the cross? The one that had welcomed Him with such acclaim when He rode into Jerusalem so triumphantly only a few days before? Had they seen Him heal the sick, make the lame walk, give sight to the blind, feed the hungry multitude who had sat listening to Him hour after hour, enraptured by His teachings? Is it these same people who now with fickle hearts suddenly turn on Him, and shout with one voice, 'Crucify him'? I am sure that the great mass of the ordinary folk who had witnessed Jesus work wonders and followed His ministry, were horrified to wake up that morning to discover it was the day of Jesus' crucifixion.

However, always on the periphery, hanging back at the edge of the crowd, were His detractors, those seeking to undermine Him, plotting and scheming His downfall, stooges of the priests, who now at His trial emerge again. They were a hostile and unforgiving crowd, hounding Him from Galilee to Golgotha.

I suspect there was a mixture of both, not those who heard Him gladly, but maybe those who had heard Him with reservation and a measure of scepticism, finding His challenges and claims too demanding, sitting on the fence, keeping all their options open. That segment of the crowd that wanted the easier option, the fickle onlookers that would rather go with the flow, maybe even hoping that one day this confidant, miracle-working Galilean preacher man might get His comeuppance. The crowd, whoever they were, were involved at three levels.

First, the crowd gave in to the expediency of the moment. They were sucked into a political manoeuvre. Pilate was desperately trying to extricate himself from his difficult position. On the evidence before him he had already decided that Jesus was an innocent man, asking, 'Why, what evil has he done?' The Luke account tells us that he put the question to them three times, so anxious was he to release Jesus. What a wonderful testimony to Jesus that neither His judge, nor His prosecutors or accusers could find any evil that He had done. Pilate was under immense pressure to placate the religious authorities who were demanding His death. If he could pass the buck to the crowd he thought it would get him off the hook by laying the responsibility on the people. The fact was that in the end it was only Pilate who had the power to condemn to death or release a prisoner. Pilate devolved his decision upon the people and the priests, by transferring the responsibility to them, and absolving himself of the guilt of Christ's blood; by washing his hands in water before them, as if the water would cleanse his guilt. He gave them the option, and the crowd made its decision. Afterwards Pilate fell into disgrace and in a few years committed suicide.*

Second, the crowd allowed themselves to be persuaded, convinced and coerced by the religious authority and political pressure. As well as manipulation from Pilate, the crowd were under pressure from the priests, who were positioning, persuading and influencing them in favour of Barabbas. They were able to manage, mislead and delude the mob into thinking he was more deserving than Jesus. They had worked feverishly in the early hours when most ordinary folk had not yet stirred from their slumbers. This is how wickedness works, in the darkness. They were pressing them urgently to have Jesus crucified. What an incredible influence was exerted on the minds of the populace in such a short space of time. By this time the priests were working the crowd, and the excited feeding frenzy was growing and now, the crowd having been urged on, 'shouted all the louder'.

Third, the crowd were swayed and caught up in the popular opinion and consensus of the moment. Not only did Pilate and the priests influence the crowd, the crowd themselves took a view. Among the citizens of Jerusalem Galileans were held in contempt and despised, and the priests had turned the claims of Jesus into pretentious ridicule in their eyes. They were now caught up in the common herd instinct. Now He was fair game,

* Source: *The International Bible Encyclopaedia* Volume Four (Eerdmans, 1939).

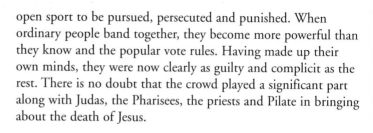

open sport to be pursued, persecuted and punished. When ordinary people band together, they become more powerful than they know and the popular vote rules. Having made up their own minds, they were now clearly as guilty and complicit as the rest. There is no doubt that the crowd played a significant part along with Judas, the Pharisees, the priests and Pilate in bringing about the death of Jesus.

In the shadow of the cross were men and women, ordinary people who had given in to the expediency of the moment, been convinced by political correctness and swayed by the popular opinion and consensus of the moment.

Discussion Starters

1. Think of other instances when Jesus drew a crowd.

_____

_____

2. What are some of the emotional factors that cause us to go along with the crowd?

_____

_____

3. What are some of the ways we endeavour to absolve our conscience?

_____

_____

4. Why do we sometimes give in to the expediency of the moment?

_____

_____

5. Is political correctness a biblical concept? Why? Why not?

_____

_____

6. Look at Daniel 3:16–18. What position did the three Hebrews take in not following political correctness?

_____

_____

7. Has anyone been swept along or got caught up in a large crowd setting? What was it like?

_____

_____

8. Has anyone gone against the crowd/popular opinion? What were the consequences?

_____

_____

Final Thoughts

How easy it is to be sucked unwittingly into the crowd, without realising the enormity of the consequences. Have you ever seen a crowd of people gathering, and out of curiosity stopped and found yourself being drawn in and maybe even swept along with them? The office sweepstake, the Christmas party, the accepted questionable practice or the grapevine rumour mill, that at the end of the day contributes to someone's demise? Someone has said that evil triumphs when good men do nothing.

Closing Prayer

Lord, I ask You to forgive me for the times when I should have stood up to be counted, when I sat and remained silent for fear of what others might think or say or do. When I stand in the awesome shadow of Your cross and again reflect on the immense price You have paid for me, I determine in my heart that, whatever the cost, I will stand for You.

For Further Study

Deuteronomy 30:19; Joshua 24:15; 1 Kings 18:21; John 6:66–69

The Roman Authorities

Self-serving Soldiers

Opening Prayer

Father, thank You for this wonderful season of Lent that enables us to be together to focus our hearts and minds afresh on Your great redemptive work. Help us to draw deeply on Your grace as our Saviour did to forgive those who treat us roughly and cause us deep pain. We are so grateful to have been recipients of Your forgiveness, may we not withhold it from others who also need to experience its transforming power. Amen.

Eye Opener

It was customary to crucify a person naked, and the soldiers on guard duty responsible for carrying out the crucifixion would strip the accused of his garments. Under the law the effects of all condemned persons were confiscated by Rome. The perk for carrying out this gruesome duty was that the four soldiers assigned to the prisoner were permitted to divide his clothes among themselves – in order to gain benefit for their value.

Icebreaker

Individually read Ephesians 6:13–17 and then describe what a Roman soldier might look like, also drawing on any other information members of the group may have picked up from other sources.

Bible Readings

John 19:16–18, 23–24, 32–34, *The Message*

Pilate caved in to their demand. He turned him over to be crucified.

They took Jesus away. Carrying his cross, Jesus went out to the place called Skull Hill (the name in Hebrew is *Golgotha*), where they crucified him, and with him two others, one on each side, Jesus in the middle ...

When they crucified him, the Roman soldiers took his clothes and divided them up four ways, to each soldier a fourth. But his robe was seamless, a single piece of weaving, so they said to each other, 'Let's not tear it up. Let's throw dice to see who gets it.' This confirmed the Scripture that said, 'They divided up my clothes among them and threw dice for my coat.' (The soldiers validated the Scriptures!) …

So the soldiers came and broke the legs of the first man crucified with Jesus, and then the other. When they got to Jesus, they saw that he was already dead, so they didn't break his legs. One of the soldiers stabbed him in the side with his spear. Blood and water gushed out.

Luke 23:36, 47, *The Message*
The soldiers also came up and poked fun at him, making a game of it. They toasted him with sour wine …

When the captain there saw what happened, he honoured God: 'This man was innocent! A good man, and innocent!'

The Self-serving Soldiers

The soldiers were also to be found in the shadow of the cross. Having led the prisoner from Pilate's judgment hall, along the Via Dolorosa to Calvary, it was their job to nail the prisoner to the gibbet. By their profession they were hard military men going about their daily work and duties, susceptible to neither fear nor pity. As they were in the act of crucifying Jesus, driving those terrible nails through His hands and feet, His response was not one of protest, but of prayer to His Father in heaven for the forgiveness of His brutal, pitiless executioners. It was not only for those ignorant heathen soldiers, it was for all who had played their part in His trial and execution and, beyond that, down through the centuries for all those who would crucify the Son of God afresh. His words were not of anger directed towards those soldiers, but of intercession and mediation directed towards His Heavenly Father for their salvation. What a response! How do we respond when others treat us badly?

Tradition suggests that the garments that had adorned the Saviour may have been made by His mother, or some of the other women. Garments that the sick had touched in faith to

receive their healing. Now they were spoils, seized upon and divided by the rough hands of army soldiers. Having taken their ill-gotten booty and divided it up among themselves, one piece remained, that was worth the most. It was His seamless undergarment, a tunic made like a long petticoat, similar to that worn by the high priests (Exod. 39:22). Not wanting to destroy its value by dividing it into four, they sat at the Saviour's feet and began to cast lots. What a desecration as these rough, coarse, scoffing, heathen soldiers now take the bloodstained garment of the Saviour and throw dice for it. What a terrible sacrilege it seems, to see them gambling in the shadow of the cross for personal gain, showing callous disregard for the Saviour hanging in anguish above them. As the crowd and priests taunted Him, the soldiers of the guard joined in and mocked Him too. It amused them to see these Jews baiting one of their own. 'If you are the King of the Jews save yourself!' they jibed as well. Suddenly their complacency and arrogant self-interest was shaken to the core. The earth rumbled and rolled, the rocks cracked and splintered and the very bowels of the earth groaned as the sun stopped shining and the sky darkened over the whole land.

The centurion (captain of 100 soldiers) who had the command of the guard, was standing closer than anyone to Jesus at this moment. Mark says the centurion 'stood there in front of Jesus'. Having ridden his horse at the head of the procession of death, that had wended its way up the Via Dolorosa, it was now his duty to remain with the sufferers to the end. On cross duty and military missions he had seen many men die, but never like this. As a Roman centurion he had witnessed courage and bravery often enough, but on this day he was witnessing something of a cataclysmic nature. As the last cry of the crucified rang out in the darkness, light as never before dawned into his soul and even though a Roman Gentile, a heathen, he could do nothing else but glorify God and make his confession of faith. This centurion was so affected that he '... praised God and said, "Surely this was a righteous man" ' (Luke 23:47).

This was the issue that had been the centre of dispute, the point on which Christ's enemies had taken Him to trial. His disciples had believed it but had been afraid to confess it, the Jews had heard it but refused to accept it. Standing on guard duty in the darkened shadow of the cross, the centurion now witnessed it and made his confession. The crucifixion of Christ had made a deep impression on his soul. There is no spirit too proud, no heart too hardened, that the power of the cross of Christ cannot humble and break. We know little more of this honest soldier, except that he was the first of countless more Gentiles who would also come to believe on the crucified Christ.

Finding Jesus already dead, and to ensure His death was beyond dispute, the soldier took his lance and forced it into the Messiah's side, thrusting between the fifth and sixth rib, piercing the pleura and stopping at the pericardium. Ordinarily the dead do not bleed, but the right auricle of the human heart can hold liquid blood after death and the outer sac a serum called hydro-pericardium. Having pierced the heart of the Saviour, John records, as the soldier withdrew his lance, blood and water gushed out. This has been explained by some medical authorities to justify that our Lord died of a broken heart. The fountain of life was pierced. Dr C. Truman Davies believes this. He says, 'We therefore have conclusive post-mortem evidence that our Lord died, not the usual crucifixion death by suffocation, but of heart failure due to the shock and constriction of the heart by fluid in the pericardium.'

According to Roman custom the bodies of those who were crucified were left hanging until the carrion birds, the dogs and other small animals reduced the corpse to bones. It was a barbarous custom, revolting to the Jews. Following the request to Pilate of Joseph of Arimathea and Nicodemus, seeking His honour and the comfort of His mother, permission was granted to remove Jesus' body. It was the legionaries and soldiers who took Him down from the cross, and we have no reason to believe they didn't handle Him carefully.

What a contrast between the Saviour and the soldiers. His only concern was forgiveness and salvation for them; they only showed disregard for Him and personal gain for themselves. To the Roman soldiers it started off as another day, another criminal, another execution. But that day, in the shadow of the cross, they witnessed the Christ of God freely forgiving, were jolted out of their self-interested indifference by a divine intervention and witnessed their captain confessing Christ to be the Son of God.

Discussion Starters

1. What do Jesus' words on forgiveness teach us?

_____

_____

_____

2. What are some of the things that people get bitter and resentful about?

_____

_____

_____

3. What are some of the emotions and life attitudes that emerge?

_____

_____

_____

4. Think of at least three Bible characters who were bitter and resentful, and three that weren't.

_____

_____

_____

5. Explore the idea of Jesus dying of a broken heart.

_____

_____

_____

6. Encourage the group to share what it took to bring them to Christ.

_____

_____

_____

7. Get the group to identify people they know who are hardened towards Christianity. Pray for them.

_____

_____

_____

Final Thoughts

Augustine once called the cross the pulpit from which Christ preached God's love to the world, while Martin Luther said that to understand the Christian message, it was necessary to start with the wounds of Christ. Johann Schroeder said, 'It has been the cross which has revealed to good men that their goodness has not been good enough.'

Closing Prayer

O God my Father, help me to remember that no matter what happens in life or how painful it may be, I can turn immediately to You knowing that as my Father You can work all things to my advantage. Keep me from all bitterness and resentment and protect my heart when others turn against me, helping me to love even as Jesus loved in His darkest hour. Amen.

For Further Study

Mark 11:25; Luke 17:4; Ephesians 4:32; Colossians 3:13; 1 John 1:9

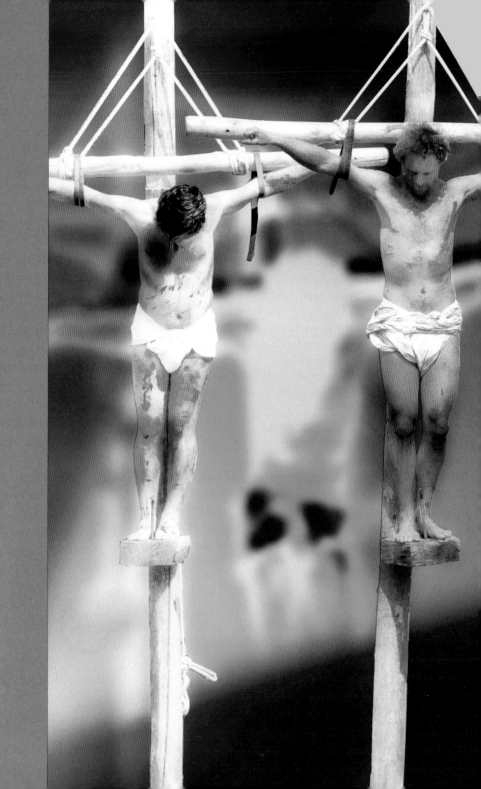

The Dying Thieves
Mocking Malefactors

Opening Prayer

Father, thank You that at this particular time of Lent we can come and contemplate the cross. As we think of You on the central cross and all that it means, we acknowledge that You didn't die alone but with two common criminals. One was responsive to You but the other resisted You. Lord, how often we have been guilty of resisting Your overtures to us when we have wanted our own way. As we come to Your Word again today, help us to be ready and willing to respond in the same way as the other thief, not to resist as the first thief did, but to be open to receive what You have to say to us. Amen.

Eye Opener

The cross occurs in at least four different forms. The first usually seen in pictures is the *crux immissa* in which there is an upright beam with a shorter crosspiece and is the most likely cross on which our Saviour died. It is the traditional form of the cross so readily seen throughout Christendom. The second, the *crux simplex*, which was probably the earliest and most primitive form, was a single beam set upright in the earth to which the victim was impaled with his hands behind him or above his head. The third was the *crux commissa* or St Anthony's cross and was formed in the shape of a letter T. The fourth was the *crux decussata*, has the shape of the letter X, and is called St Andrew's cross because tradition has it that the brother of Peter was crucified upside down on this type of cross. The cross itself was not a lofty erection – much lower than it is portrayed in Christian art, leaving the prisoner hanging quite near the ground, meaning that in the midst of His last agonies, Jesus was all the more exposed to the jeers, insults and taunts of the bystanders and passers-by.

Icebreaker

Imagine you have been mugged and in the process were relieved of your watch and some cash by the assailant. You were left bleeding, bruised and badly shaken up. Some months pass, your assailant is

apprehended, and you have the opportunity of a face-to-face confrontation. What might you be feeling when you meet your assailant and what might you want to say?

Bible Reading
Luke 23:39–43

One of the criminals who hung there hurled insults at him: 'Aren't you the Christ? Save yourself and us!'

But the other criminal rebuked him. 'Don't you fear God,' he said, 'since you are under the same sentence? We are punished justly, for we are getting what our deeds deserve. But this man has done nothing wrong.'

Then he said, 'Jesus, remember me when you come into your kingdom.'

Jesus answered him, 'I tell you the truth, today you will be with me in paradise.'

The Mocking Malefactors

There were shadows cast by three crosses that day and it's quite possible that as the sun moved round, the shadow of the central cross fell upon the other two. Whether it did or not, we do know that by their responses to Him the malefactors – wicked men – recognised they were in the presence of the Saviour.

Crucifixion was a common form of execution. It was where the worst people of the land ended their days. As they awaited their turn, these two criminals had witnessed the soldiers hammering and driving in the terrible nails that impaled the Son of God to a Roman gibbet. The searing pain and flowing blood had not evoked the usual torrent of curses and blasphemies and, although in great agony, with strength of resolve and great compassion for those brutal, pitiless murderers, they had heard Him breath out, 'Father, forgive them, for they do not know what they are doing.'

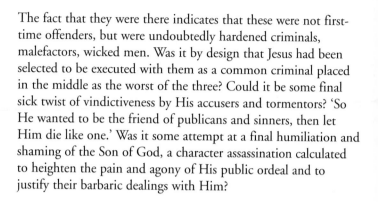

The fact that they were there indicates that these were not first-time offenders, but were undoubtedly hardened criminals, malefactors, wicked men. Was it by design that Jesus had been selected to be executed with them as a common criminal placed in the middle as the worst of the three? Could it be some final sick twist of vindictiveness by His accusers and tormentors? 'So He wanted to be the friend of publicans and sinners, then let Him die like one.' Was it some attempt at a final humiliation and shaming of the Son of God, a character assassination calculated to heighten the pain and agony of His public ordeal and to justify their barbaric dealings with Him?

How foolish people are in thinking they can outwit the Almighty. This particular scenario in Christ's sufferings had been foreseen by the Old Testament prophet Isaiah (53:12) – that He should be numbered with the transgressors.

The pathway they had travelled to the cross can only be surmised. Had they come from deprived backgrounds or bad homes? Had they come from good homes, but fallen in with bad company at an early age? Had they left behind broken-hearted parents or bruised and battered victims? Whatever their past, they were now faced with the presence of a righteous Saviour.

There were three crosses with shadows that day, each conveying a particular response to the unfolding drama. The first robber's response was one of derision and rebellion. Staying true to his life of self-interest and self-preservation, in sneering, mocking tones he bellows out, 'Aren't you the Christ, then save yourself and us as well.' His tone and attitude were so hostile and aggressive, that even his partner in crime could not bear to see the Son of God spoken to in that way. 'We deserve what we've got,' he chided, 'but this man has done nothing wrong.'

What an opportunity was missed that day, as the sneering thief's mind was so blinded to the possibilities that were before him in Christ. He wanted to use the Son of God as an escape route from the predicament and consequences of his own actions. There was no willingness for change, just the opportunity to try and take advantage of the goodness of God to serve his own personal ends. No regret, no remorse, no shame, just the arrogance of a self-seeking heart, riding roughshod over the mercy and grace of a loving Saviour.

What a contrast from the other robber. Not rebellion and derision, but repentance and desire. He may have come by the same route, hardened by crime and sin, but in these moments of realisation his heart was strangely moved. He had seen something in the Nazarene that had given him hope.

Maybe he had heard the stories of Jesus and was now encountering for the first time the Son of God for himself. Even though he was a bad man, he feared God and knew a great travesty was being perpetrated before his very eyes. Putting his pride to one side, he publicly called on the Name of Jesus before the on-looking crowd. 'Jesus,' he cried, 'Jesus, remember me when you come into your kingdom.' This was the cry of a penitent man, not arrogant with self-interest and self-preservation, but a man willing to acknowledge his own sinfulness, to acknowledge the Son of God and to ask to be included in His kingdom. The prayer of a dying sinner to a dying Saviour.

Jesus, occupying the third cross, the central cross, responds to the man's repentance and desire with redemption and deliverance. Jesus answered and said, 'I tell you the truth, today you will be with me in paradise.' Only the cross of Christ is the cross of redemption and deliverance. In those dying moments Jesus responded with deep compassion and great grace, reaching out to a penitent heart and a contrite spirit. The dying man was saved at the last gasp. Thank God that whatever our past failure and sin may have been, we can move from a cross of rebellion, by way of a cross of repentance, to kneel in the shadow of the cross of redemption, receiving forgiveness and grace, knowing that our future in Christ is assured. It is never too late.

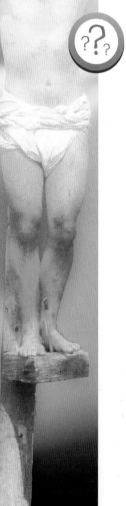

Model of a penitent heart
- Distanced himself from his sinful companion. Luke 23:40
- Confessed his own sinfulness. Luke 23:41
- Expressed the fear of God. Luke 23:41
- Proclaimed Christ to be the sinless one. Luke 23:41
- Confessed the Name of Jesus. Luke 23:42
- Prayed a simple prayer of faith. Luke 23:42
- Received the immediate answer to his prayer of faith. Luke 23:43

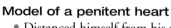

Discussion Starters

1. Crucifixion was an ugly form of punishment and death. Discuss briefly the different types of cross.

_____
_____
_____
_____

2. The scripture says that one of the criminals, 'hurled insults at Christ'. What are some of the insults hurled at Christ and His followers today? How can we deal with them?

_____
_____
_____
_____

3. Discuss how the first thief displayed rebellion and derision and how it can manifest itself. Discuss the contrast of the two thieves' responses.

_____
_____
_____
_____
_____

4. Discuss 'the fear of God' in the way the thief used the phrase to rebuke his compatriot in crime.

_____
_____
_____
_____

5. What do you think he meant when he said, 'Jesus, remember me when you come into your kingdom'?

_____
_____
_____
_____

6. Why do desire and repentance go together? What does repentance really mean?

_____
_____
_____
_____

7. Jesus experienced joy in the midst of pain and suffering. What does this teach us about being other-centred?

_____
_____
_____
_____

Final Thoughts

Both criminals had the opportunity to change their cross for a crown; one turned his back on the opportunity, but the other grasped it with both outstretched hands. There are people like that today, who find themselves on a cross of affliction of their own making, who are bitter and angry, blaming others and God, spurning the chance of grace, bemoaning their pain and anguish by crucifying themselves further on a cross of rebellion. Others, like the penitent criminal, can sum up their experience in the words of the old hymn writer William Cowper.

> *The dying thief rejoiced to see that fountain in his day;*
> *And there may I, though vile as he, wash all my sins away.*
> *I do believe, I will believe, that Jesus died for me!*
> *That on the cross He shed His blood, from sin to set me free.*

The apostle Paul sums up the scenario of the three crosses for us when he says, 'For the message of the cross is foolishness to those who are perishing, but to us who are being saved it is the power of God' (1 Cor. 1:18).

Closing Prayer

Thank you, Father, for allowing Your Son, the King of Glory, to be crucified with common criminals and in so doing to identify with the likes of me, a common sinner. Thank You, Lord, also, that through Your love and great sacrifice You have overcome my suspicions and rebellion. I thank You that the shadow of Your cross has fallen on my life, and I come again and reaffirm my faith in You, turn from my sinful ways and, like the dying thief, embrace afresh the assurance of forgiveness and the knowledge of a certain future.

For Further Study

Psalm 95:7–8; Proverbs 28:14; 29:1; Isaiah 55:7; Romans 2:5;
2 Corinthians 7:10; Hebrews 3:13

The Faithful Followers

Compassionate Carers

Opening Prayer

Lord, as we continue to contemplate the cross and Your willingness to go that way for us, we ask that You will help us to take up our cross and follow You. May Your Holy Spirit bring fresh insight and understanding to us today as we continue to consider the lives of those who gathered in the shadow of the cross. Help us to be open to each other and to You, as we share in this Bible study together. In Jesus' Name we ask. Amen

Eye Opener

The word cross is derived from the Latin word *crux*, from which we get the word ex*cruci*ate, meaning to experience the torment and torture of the most severe, unbearable, agonising, intense, extreme pain. The suffering of death by crucifixion was particularly intense, especially in hot climates. Severe local inflammation, coupled with significant bleeding of the jagged wounds, produced a traumatic fever which was aggravated by the exposure to the heat of the sun, the strained position of the body and insufferable thirst. The wound swelled about the rough nails and the torn and lacerated tendons and nerves caused excruciating agony. The arteries of the head and stomach were surcharged with blood and a terrific throbbing headache ensued. Tetanus and the rigours of the attending convulsions would tear at the wounds and add to the burden of pain, till at last the bodily forces were exhausted and the victim sank to unconsciousness and death. The victims of crucifixion literally died a thousand deaths. The length of this agony was wholly determined by the constitution of the victim, but death rarely ensued before 36 hours had elapsed. The sudden death of Christ evidently was a matter of surprise and astonishment (Mark 15:44).

Icebreaker

Get each person to write out a definition of the concept 'to minister to someone', listing practical ways of implementing and demonstrating care. Put the group in twos to share, then take reflections of the group by sharing.

Bible Readings

Matthew 27:32–34; 48, 55, *The Message*

Along the way they came on a man from Cyrene named Simon and made him carry Jesus' cross. Arriving at Golgotha, the place they call 'Skull Hill,' they offered him a mild painkiller (a mixture of wine and myrrh), but when he tasted it he wouldn't drink it …

Some bystanders who heard him said, 'He's calling for Elijah.' One of them ran and got a sponge soaked in sour wine and lifted it on a stick so he could drink. The others joked, 'Don't be in such a hurry. Let's see if Elijah comes and saves him.' …

There were also quite a few women watching from a distance, women who had followed Jesus from Galilee in order to serve him. Among them were Mary Magdalene, Mary the mother of James and Joseph, and the mother of the Zebedee brothers.

John 19:26–27, *The Message*

While the soldiers were looking after themselves, Jesus' mother, his aunt, Mary the wife of Clopas, and Mary Magdalene stood at the foot of the cross. Jesus saw his mother and the disciple he loved standing near her. He said to his mother, 'Woman, here is your son.' Then to the disciple, 'Here is your mother.' From that moment the disciple accepted her as his own mother.

The Compassionate Carers

On one occasion, Jesus was asked, 'Who is my neighbour?' and responded with the account of a man who was beaten, robbed and left to die. Those who should have cared, a priest and a Levite (religious men), walked by on the other side. It was, instead, the unlikely response of a Samaritan traveller, who

reached out that day and ministered to the dying man. Was this story a foreshadowing of the cross?

On the cross we see a man beaten, robbed of His dignity and left to die, with the priests, Levites and religious leaders baying for His blood. When it seemed the tide of the world had turned against Him, a small and steady stream of compassion flowed towards the cross, caught in small glimpses, in acts and words of kindness and deeds of compassion. They helped to let Him know that not all the bystanders were cruel and callous, there were those cared.

The burden-bearer: There is no more harrowing a sight, than the tragic procession to Calvary of Christ, staggering, swaying, stumbling and falling under the weight of the Roman gibbet. Weakened and drained of strength by the ordeal of His trial and flogging, the contempt and cruelty of His tormentors and the open wounds of his bleeding back, slowly, exhausted, He grinds to a halt and sinks to the ground under the weight and enormity of the burden. Fearing that He might die before His final humiliation, they pressgang a bystander to carry His cross, a Libyan Jew called Simon. Luke says that they laid the cross on him. Whether he wanted to carry it or not, we do not know, but there is no indication that he protested or demurred from this onerous task.

Seeing the bloodied, beaten, exhausted Jesus must have stirred some compassion in his heart and that day Simon lightened the physical load of the Son of God, and became the burden-bearer.

The benevolent ministers: It seems that a kind of guild or association of benevolent and charitable women, a compassionate sisterhood, had established itself in Jerusalem. In order to dull the senses and lessen the intensity of the pain crucifixion inflicted, these women offered and administered to those facing crucifixion a partly drugged wine to deaden the pain. This was offered before the condemned were nailed to the cross to act as an opiate to stupefy the senses and render a measure of insensibility to the pain and pangs of a slow and difficult death. It was a mixture of a vinegar wine mixed with myrrh and gall, a particularly bitter and sour mix. It was an act of mercy which the Romans permitted. Some think it may have been offered by the soldiers. As Jesus came to Calvary, they offered it to Him to drink, but after tasting it, He declined. He was unwilling to blunt the pains of dying, cloud His mind or dull the awareness of His circumstances.

In the Garden of Gethsemane He had picked up the cup of suffering, which His Father had given Him and drunk from that cup. His refusal was not a rebuttal or rejection of the concern and compassion demonstrated, but His focus was on a higher purpose. The intention and purpose behind it would have cheered His heart – it was the very demonstration of His teaching on the Good Samaritan.

The courageous man: As the hours of crucifixion dragged on, the immense pain and anguish was aggravated by the exposure to the heat of the sun and an insufferable thirst ensued. So much so, that the Son of God cried out, 'I thirst.' This was the only cry of physical torment to pass the lips of the dying Saviour, thus fulfilling the prophetic insight of the psalmist David (Psa. 69:21). As others ignored His plea, a man, maybe a soldier, who could bear the spectacle no longer, suddenly darted forward with a sponge on the stem of a hyssop and moistened Jesus' parched lips. Someone, willing to stand out and go against the tide and mood of the moment, had ignored the hostile, taunting crowd and, not daunted or intimidated, reached out to the Son of God. In the midst of the darkness he brought a ray of light, in the face of hostility an act of kindness, of human tenderness, in the presence of deep hatred a moment of compassion and in the shadow of the cross an act of great courage.

The faithful followers: This group of holy women were faithful followers of Jesus and now, horrified by the events they were witnessing, they stood a little distance from the cross,

undoubtedly overwhelmed by their sense of revulsion and disbelief and trying to come to terms with the horrendous fate of the One they so deeply loved and worshipped. They stood there helpless, unable to do anything, but they were determined to be there in the Saviour's hour of greatest need.

In the midst of this baying, howling, fiendish rabble, there were those faithful followers who, because of their love, were with Him to the end, and by their very presence, would minister strength, comfort and support to the Saviour as He looked upon them from the cross. Despite the shame and ignominy, unable to look on His broken naked form as the crowd gazed and gawped and sneered, they remained steadfast to the bitter end. I am grateful also for this group of dedicated women who sustained my Lord to the last.

The loyal friend and loving family: Where were the men we might ask? Those He spent His days and nights with, pouring His soul and heart into, teaching training and to whom He revealed the kingdom of God. Surely they would be here to defend His honour and stand up for His cause? After all He had prepared them for this day. Unfortunately, they were found wanting. Some had slept in the garden when He had faced His severest test. One had betrayed Him with a kiss, another had denied and disowned Him with a curse. One would doubt Him with cynicism and some would walk away and return to their old familiar haunts, while yet others would be found hiding and cowering in fear of their lives.

As Jesus looked down from the cross, His eyes scanning and searching the crowd for 'His men', they were nowhere to be found. Except for John, he was there, his memory wasn't short, he was not found wanting – on the contrary, stalwart and supporting at the side of Jesus' stricken, quivering heartbroken mother in the hours of her greatest distress. What a comfort to Jesus to see the most important woman in His life, this devout God-fearing saintly mother, strengthened and succoured by the disciple whom He loved. Knowing He could depend on the loyalty of a devoted disciple and trusted friend who was there, not only for Him, but also consoling His mother on this tumultuous day must have given Him deep comfort and strength. To John He gave the awesome privilege and solemn charge from the cross to care for His mother.

Discussion Starters

1. Crucifixion was a particularly gruesome form of punishment and death that could take as long as three days to take its full course. Discuss why the sudden death of Christ evidently was a matter of astonishment (Mark 15:44).

_____
_____
_____
_____

2. Look again at the account of the Good Samaritan and draw out the various elements that he displayed in demonstrating compassion (Luke 10:25–37).

_____
_____
_____
_____

3. In what ways can we follow Simon's example and carry out a practical ministry of burden-bearing?

_____
_____
_____
_____
_____
_____

4. The concerned women wanted to alleviate the suffering and pain of others in their hour of need and shame. Share ideas about ways we can help to alleviate personal pain as well as the practical ministry of burden-bearing.

_____

_____

_____

_____

5. What is the greatest thirst in the world and what did Jesus say about satisfying it? How can we become courageous men and women who are willing to step from the crowd with living water?

_____

_____

_____

_____

6. Faithfulness and loyalty are demonstrated in different ways. Identify some of them and think of some other biblical examples.

_____

_____

_____

_____

7. Friendship is not easy to find or establish. The psalmist said, 'Look to my right and see; no-one is concerned for me. I have no refuge; no one cares for my life.' What are the qualities of friendship?

_____

_____

_____

_____

Final Thoughts

There were those who deserted the cross because they were wiped out by the shame and disgrace of it all. There were those who revelled in using the cross to amplify the shame of others. There were those who were shamed by its awfulness, but because of their commitment, love and devotion were not ashamed of their Saviour. They stood strongly in its shadow forgoing the shame and ridicule of the crowd and identifying with the Son of God. Are you ashamed of the cross or are you its defender?

Closing Prayer

Lord, so often we miss the opportunity to show a kindness to someone along the way, to speak a word of encouragement to someone who is struggling or to champion the cause of the underprivileged. As we have considered those today who ministered to You from the shadow of the cross, may it motivate and inspire us to reach out a helping hand to others in their hour of need. To be there for them, when it seems the world has turned against them, to carry the burden with them when they fall beneath its load. To be willing to speak up for them when they have no voice, and to provide support for their family needs. Lord, I am grateful for those who ministered to You in Your hour of greatest need. May I not be found wanting as some were, but willing to be there when needed.

For Further Study

Mark 15:21–23; 36–40; Luke 23:26, 49; John 19:25–29

Seeking Soul
Were You There?

Opening Prayer

Heavenly Father, we come together for our last Lent study on the cross. We have looked at what the shadow of the cross meant for others, and we pray that today You will open our eyes to grasp what the cross means for us. Give us ears to hear Your voice and open hearts to receive Your Word. In Jesus' Name we ask. Amen.

Eye Opener

As I write, an article in today's newspaper draws attention to the fact that the current 'must have' fashion accessory is a cross. It says: 'There is a spreading fashion of wearing crosses decorated with diamonds and other precious stones that has become the mania of the moment. Crosses glitter around the necks of soubrettes, TV personalities, leading models and actresses. To Christians it is a sacred symbol of self-sacrifice, but to a growing band of rich and famous celebrities who favour the flamboyantly displayed, diamond encrusted variety, it is little more than self-adornment. Is it relevant to the gospel to spend thousands of pounds to buy a sacred symbol of Christianity and then, perhaps in an unchristian manner, forget those that suffer and die of hunger in the world?' (James Mills, *Daily Mail*, 23 May 2002)

Icebreaker

Take the image of the cross and some bread and wine and spend a few minutes looking at it. What does it symbolise for each of you? Where are some of the places you have seen the symbol of the cross displayed other than a church? How do you feel about the use of the cross in fashion?

Bible Readings
Isaiah 53:3–6

He was despised and rejected by men, a man of sorrows, and familiar with suffering. Like one from whom men hide their faces he was despised, and we esteemed him not.

Surely he took up our infirmities and carried our sorrows, yet we considered him stricken by God, smitten by him, and afflicted. But he was pierced for our transgressions, he was crushed for our iniquities; the punishment that brought us peace was upon him, and by his wounds we are healed. We all, like sheep, have gone astray, each of us has turned to his own way; and the Lord has laid on him the iniquity of us all.

1 Corinthians 1:18, *The Message*

The Message that points to Christ on the Cross seems like sheer silliness to those hellbent on destruction, but for those on the way of salvation it makes perfect sense. This is the way God works, and most powerfully as it turns out.

Were You There?

We have been considering some of those who found themselves standing in the shadow of the cross. The cross is the symbol or sign that signifies the reality of what took place 2,000 years ago at Calvary. A once-for-all happening in history, never to be repeated or superseded, and in that sense we were not there, but be sure of this, we were represented there.

Some people idolise and enshrine the cross, gold-plating it as a spiritual icon or using it as an ornament or piece of jewellery. Others venerate it in stained-glass windows or on the altar as a memorial. Others despise it, even burn it, treating it with derision and disdain.

However, it stands stark against the backdrop of history and eternity, speaking across the centuries with a clear message to all humanity that cannot be ignored. Every man or woman, sooner or later is confronted with its reality, because its power reaches down the generations and speaks across the centuries to you and I today. The power and meaning of the cross never changes.

The cross has come to represent many things, but above all its purpose was for one thing only: death. What then does the death of Jesus mean, and the cross therefore signify? Why did Jesus die? He was in the prime of life, at the height of popularity with widespread influence. It was not the death of a suicide. Others took His life which He voluntarily laid down. It was no accidental death, but deliberate murder. It was not the death of a criminal. Even the Roman soldier declared, 'Surely this is a righteous man,' and Pilate declared, 'I find no fault in Him.' Some have suggested that His death was the death of a martyr, but Jesus did not simply die for a good cause as others have done. The only adequate explanation of the death of Jesus on the cross of Calvary, is that His life was given in death willingly, as a sacrifice for sin. It is the place where sin collides with love and righteousness.

The consequence of sin is death. The Scriptures declare that, 'without the shedding of blood there is no forgiveness' (Heb. 9:22). Throughout the Old Testament continual sacrifice was made to atone for the sins of the people, but the blood of bulls and goats had been insufficient. There needed to be a once-and-for-all sacrifice to pay the price for sin, yours and mine, and on that cross He became our sin-bearer. We may not have been there in person, but the hatred, wickedness and deceit of our own hearts as expressed in the lives of others in the shadow of the cross was atoned for in that great act of sacrifice. It was through His death that the full penalty of sin was paid.

The cross is witness to the fact that it was sin in all its ugliness that killed the Son of God, striking at the very heart of God with anguish, pain and the depths of sorrow. Sin had failed to destroy His character, or nullify His ministry, but it put Him to death. All the shame, the insult, suffering, pain and grisly agony seen at the cross is the handiwork of sin. He bore the full weight of it alone upon that cross, exposed and helpless to the crushing of sin's full hate and malice. The moment came, He could bear it no more, His heart breaking under its weight and power. 'It is finished,' He cries and as the torture of His spirit and the agony of His soul touch the limit of human endurance, He says, 'Father, into your hands I commit my spirit.' The price was paid once and for all.

You and I must also make this journey to the shadow of the cross and allow our own sinful hearts to be deeply moved. Some will survey the cross and walk away calling its message foolishness, others will have eyes to see a love so amazing, so divine, that it demands their soul, their life, their all. It must become more than just an event of ancient history, we must enter into the reality, wonder and living power of its redemptive work. It is in its shadow that the depths of our sin is revealed and exposed, the depth of His love expressed, and the joy of reconciliation experienced. As the old hymn writer put it:

> *We may not know we cannot tell*
> *What pains He had to bear;*
> *But we believe it was for us*
> *He hung and suffered there.*
>
> *He died that we might be forgiven*
> *He died to make us good,*
> *That we might go at last heaven*
> *Saved by His precious blood.*
>
> *There was no other good enough*
> *To pay the price of sin:*
> *He only could unlock the gate*
> *Of heaven, and let us in.*
>
> C.F. Alexander

As we stand in the shadow of the cross, it exposes us for who we are. We cannot be saved by looking at the cross, venerating it or wearing it as a piece of jewellery, but by allowing the Holy Spirit to apply to our lives the redemptive work that was wrought through it. The sins that nailed Christ to the wood were the same sins that you and I have committed. In that sense I can truly and shamefully say that I played my part along with the rest. I was there when they crucified my Lord.

The cross stands as a testimony to the devilish worst that man sought to do to God, but gloriously demonstrates the length and breadth that God in His love will go to for man. Come to the cross today, to remind yourself of the price that was paid, that the cross is now empty and that all Jesus made available through it is available to us. Jesus declared, 'But I, when I am lifted up from the earth, will draw all men to myself' (John 12:32), and that includes both you and me.

Discussion Starters

1. Which of the characters around the cross do you identify with most? Why?

_____

_____

_____

_____

2. Looking back over the weeks, what has affected you the most?

_____

_____

_____

_____

3. What emotions have you experienced as you have considered those who stood in the shadow of the cross?

_____

_____

_____

_____

4. In what ways can you help others feel the impact of the shadow of the cross?

_____

_____

_____

_____

5. What do you feel now about the sacrifice of the Saviour?

_____

_____

_____

_____

6. If someone asked you, 'What is the meaning of the cross?' how might you answer?

_____

_____

_____

_____

7. What personal challenge to change has the study brought to you?

_____

_____

_____

_____

Final Thoughts

Take some moments to visit the cross once again, contemplating its meaning and gazing upon its emptiness, recognising that Jesus gave Himself to save and to bless others. What a terrible thing sin is that it required such sacrifice. How can we go on sinning so carelessly when we recognise what our Saviour suffered to redeem us from our sins? Come now and stand in the shadow of an empty cross and, in moments of reflection confess your sin and, in an act of deep repentance, embrace the forgiveness so freely available. Let your heart rise in wonder, love and praise for the price that was paid and the gift of salvation that has been given, echoing the words of another great old hymn: 'I take, O cross, Thy shadow, for my abiding place.'

Closing Prayer

Give me a sight, O Saviour, of your wondrous love to me:
Of the love that brought you down to earth, to die on Calvary.
Was it the nails O Saviour, that bound you to the tree?
No, it was your everlasting love, your love for me, for me.
Oh wonder of all wonders, that through your death for me,
My open sins, my secret sins, can all forgiven be!
Then melt my heart O Saviour, bend me, yes, break me down,
Until I own you conqueror, and Lord and Sovereign crown.

Oh, make me understand it, help me to take it in;
What it meant to you the Holy One to bear away my sin.
Amen

Katharine A.M. Kelly

For Further Study

1 Corinthians 1:17; Galatians 6:14; Ephesians 2:16;
Colossians 1:20

Leader's Notes

Study 1 **The Pharisees and Priests**

Icebreaker

Get people to remember and articulate as much as they can. Select three people to read from *The Message* version, Luke 18:9–14; one taking the narration, one the position of the Pharisee and one the taxman.

Discussion Starters

1. The core issue to underline is that they were more concerned with religious rituals, the accuracy of inconsequential detail and external appearances. Draw out what Jesus considered to be the basics: fairness, compassion and commitment.

2. Religious bigotry seeks to impose on others' standards, rules and requirements, evidenced by dogmatic intolerance and dismissal of their viewpoint. Principled convictions are cherished attitudes and values, a standard for personal conduct, based on integrity and honour, respecting others' viewpoints even though you disagree with them.

3. Draw examples from: the business world, for example, corporate companies making excess profit to the detriment of the consumer; the political world, for example, the spin and economy with the truth; and the religious world, for example, the lack of real involvement with social issues.

4. Jesus was exposing their lack of moral integrity, as well as challenging their superiority complex, their position of false standing and their comfort zone, Draw out the fact that in His presence they felt threatened in the self-righteous pattern of life they had become familiar and comfortable with.

5. Ask the group to share some personal experiences of how they were antagonistic to the gospel, and see if they can identify with the Pharisees' response to Jesus.

6. You are looking to draw out things like: wanting to present a good image, holding bigoted opinions, being self-righteous about our own high standards, being unaccepting and intolerant of others who don't hold our values, having double standards etc.

7. Self-righteousness is having an exaggerated awareness of one's own virtuousness and importance. Being holier than thou with a false piety and sanctimonious, self-satisfied, smug, superior attitude. It manifests itself by pride. The icebreaker is the classic biblical example.

8. Pride has a least four effects. It gives us an inflated sense of our own importance, it looks on others with disdain and contempt, it actively puts others down and demeans them, and it results in a haughty arrogance.

Study 2 **The Common People**

Icebreaker

The object here is to get group members' responses to what is popularly accepted as a harmless indulgence. Get the group to explore and share their responses to the note.

Discussion Starters

1. Telling parables at the lakeside (Matt. 13), healing the blind men at Jericho (Matt. 20), the healing of the woman with an issue of blood (Mark 5), at Decapolis, the healing of the deaf and mute man (Mark 7), the man at the pool of Bethesda (John 5).

2. Draw these out from the group, such as: fear of rejection, fear of ridicule, the need to be accepted, not wanting to stand out or be the odd man out. Not being able to face disapproval or confrontation.

3. We can learn to be sensitive and responsive to conscience or we can choose to ignore it and allow it to become dulled, going along with the crowd. People deal with a troubled conscience by religious compensation, good works, a denial of reality, rationalisation and even a re-evaluation of convictions.

4. Often because it is convenient to do so and the price for not doing so is too high to pay. Sometimes for personal gain, advancement, personal pleasure or because we are too weak to resist and put up a fight. Draw out from the group what expediency means – basically looking after our own interests rather than doing what is fair and just and right (1 Cor. 10:23).

5. Draw the group out to differentiate between sensitivity to an individual's personal rights and dignity and compromise on matters of moral integrity and justice. Discuss how Pilate may have been politically correct, but morally lacking.

6. Get someone to read the account. They were not willing to compromise convictions and faith in order to retain privileged positions. They believed God was able to save them from the consequences of their stand, 'but if not', they would still not compromise either to save their prestigious positions or their own skin.

7. Get members of the group to share if they have attended a large gathering of people, like a football match, concert, or vastly crowded street or airport where they were caught in the flow of the crowd. How did they feel?

8. Explore with the group times when they have stood up and been counted. What were the issues? Why did they feel so strongly about them? What sort of responses did they get? And how did they deal with them.

Study 3 **The Roman Authorities**

Icebreaker

The goal here is to create a visual image of a Roman soldier. *Helmet* made of metal over a leather ring; *Breastplate* made of chain mail overlapping moulded metal plates; *Shield* made of wood covered with skin, with metal surround and central plate, round, oval or oblong in shape; *Sword* about 20 inches long, broad and two-edged; *Spear* 7 feet long, light wood tipped with barbed iron; *Greaves* worn only by centurions as a sign of distinction, were metal shin pads that also covered the knees.

Discussion Starters

1. Jesus' thoughts in the midst of overwhelmingly painful circumstances were not towards Himself. No self-pity, or self-concern. He remained other-centred; His thoughts were towards the needs of His executioners and trust in His Father. He did not ask 'Why me Lord?' His first focus was 'Father' and His second 'Forgive'.

2. You are looking for the group members to share life experiences, such as deep disappointments, being hurt by others, cheated by a business partner, lacking love from a parent etc.

3. Emotions such as hostility, anger, distrust, anxiety, fear. Life patterns such as self-protection, criticism of others, being self-absorbed, negative responses, living in the past, reliving and retelling old issues.

4. Examples of some who were: Simon (Acts 8:23), Jonah, Cain, Esau. And some who weren't: Job, Joseph, Paul.

5. People's hearts break because of unrequited love and unbearable rejection. Jesus came to His own and they rejected Him. He looked over Jerusalem and wept. One disciple betrayed Him, one doubted and one denied. The crowd deserted Him, the soldiers cruelly crucified Him, His Father couldn't watch, Jesus cried, 'My God, my God, why have you forsaken me?'

6. Get people to share their testimonies, recognising that some will not be dramatic but more a gradual awareness and commitment to Christ

7. Spend time praying for people mentioned and encourage group members to invite them to an Easter service, Easter activity or for a meal together.

Study 4 **The Dying Thieves**

Icebreaker

Break the group down into twos or threes. Get them to identify some of the feelings they may have experienced during the ordeal itself, and some of the feelings at the prospect of, and in the process of confronting their assailant. Get them to express what they might want to say to their attacker and take feedback into the main group.

Discussion Starters

1. Crucifixion was a Roman not Jewish punishment. The footrest shown by most artists is not historical or even probable. A wedge or crutch, which Tertullian describes as being like a rhinoceros horn, was placed between the legs of the victim causing additional agony.

2. Explore what sort of insults or nicknames group members may have been targeted with because of their faith. Identify some of the more general ways insults are targeted at Christ, like taking the Lord's name in vain or portraying Christ as a homosexual in poetry and films.

3. This man did not want to be delivered from his sins but their consequences. He wanted to be saved not through the cross, but from it. Derision goes a step further and ridicules, mocks, scoffs, scorns and disparages the other person. Wasn't he really saying in his taunt, 'You're not the Christ, otherwise you'd be saving yourself and us'?

4. The word fear is used in the sense of awe. One thief treated Christ with contempt, the other with a deep sense of awe and reverence, recognising who He was. Reflect on the ways in which the fear of God can be shown, such as, obedience, forgiveness, love.

5. It is clear that the thief knew he was about to die, but that there was an afterlife. Jesus was the One who was able to usher him into this kingdom. Explore with the group what the kingdom of God is. Look at Matthew 13. On six occasions in this chapter Jesus said, 'The kingdom of heaven is like …'

6. Repentance is an act of the will and decision of the mind. If there is no desire for change, there will be no commitment to it. Desire is the want to change and repentance the willingness to make the change. Use the model of the penitent heart to define repentance.

7. Though Christ was in great agony, He had a word of comfort, hope and assurance to speak to the penitent. As in life, so in death. Closeted with a seeking soul, be it Nicodemus, the woman at the well, Zacchaeus, or the blind man who cried 'Son of David, have mercy on me', He was other-centred to the last.

Study 5 The Faithful Followers

Icebreaker

Take reflections from the group and keep the concept ministry as broad as possible, to include preaching, the ministry gifts, deacons etc. (Rom. 12:3–8; 1 Cor. 12:27–28). Then explore what the ministry of caring is.

Discussion Starters

1. Jesus' life was not slowly squeezed out of Him, from suffocation. John says He gave His life with the triumphant words, 'It is finished' (John 19:30). Note, not 'I am finished'. It was the great work of redemption that had been accomplished by the great Sin-Bearer, and once it had been done He breathed His last breath. He had finished the work his Father had given Him to do.

2. There are at least ten things the Samaritan did. Break the group down into twos or threes to identify them. Get each group to reflect a couple back into the main group.

3. Paul exhorted the Galatians, 'Carry each other's burdens, and in this way you will fulfil the law of Christ' (Gal. 6:2). Explore with the group what might be some burdens people need help with, for example, children, finances, decorating, the need for a break etc.

4. Pain comes to all of us in different ways. Explore with the group the different ways people experience pain such as loneliness, rejection, betrayal, loss, unrequited love etc. Ask the question, how can we minister to people in their moments of pain.

5. The psalmist said, 'My soul thirsts for God, for the living God.' Isaiah said, 'Come, all you who are thirsty, come to the waters.' Jesus said, 'If anyone is thirsty, let him come to me and drink' (John 7:37). Spend some moments in prayer asking God for courage to step out from the crowd to offer this water to the thirsty.

6. You are looking for responses such as: Devoted, dependable, reliable, loyal, true. Those who are not faithful are disloyal, fickle, unreliable, changeable. Examples of loyalty: David and Jonathan, Ruth and Naomi, Elijah and Elisha, John the beloved and Jesus, Paul and Timothy, Priscilla and Aquila.

7. Bring out some of the following points. A true friend will accept, affirm and encourage; will always be there for you; does not display judgmental attitudes; always keeps the lines of communication open; will concentrate on positive qualities, without ignoring negative ones; is honest enough to share faults with you. A true friend conveys an attitude of openness, honesty and trust; is loyal to the end.

Study 6 **A Seeking Soul**

Icebreaker

Take responses from the group, leaving the cross, bread and wine in a prominent position. At the end of this evening's study, finish by sharing the bread and wine together.

Discussion Starters

1. Ask the group to break into twos to reflect on the different characters in the study and to talk through whom they most identify with. Take feedback into the main group from those who want to share.

2. Recognise people will share at different levels. Some may have been affected emotionally, others by a deep spiritual challenge and some by fresh insight or new perspectives. Be sensitive and supportive.

3. These might include thankfulness, gratitude, shame, guilt, awe, wonder, love, anger as well as others. Explore these together and encourage the group to share why they think they may have felt the emotion. Don't press them if they are reluctant.

4. The cross is not a concept, but a reality that can be demonstrated by the way we live. Draw out from the carers round the cross how the shadow of the cross upon us will cause us to reach out to others.

6. You are looking to draw out such things as: Christ's sacrifice for sin, forgiveness, mercy, love, grace, reconciliation, the power of eternal life – that it provides all we need to live.

7. Based on the studies, ask each group member to take a pen and piece of paper and jot down the salient points they might focus on in response to the question. Give them about ten minutes and then ask some of them to share with the group.

Finish with a time of sharing bread and wine, but ask the group to spend a few moments in prayer asking the Holy Spirit to bring to mind challenges they may have felt during the course of the Lent study. Encourage them to settle any issues of the heart as they take the bread and wine.

National Distributors

UK: (and countries not listed below)
CWR, Waverley Abbey House, Waverley Lane, Farnham,
Surrey GU9 8EP.
Tel: (01252) 784710 Outside UK (44) 1252 784710

AUSTRALIA: CMC Australasia, PO Box 519, Belmont,
Victoria 3216.
Tel: (03) 5241 3288

CANADA: Cook Communications Ministries, PO Box 98, 55
Woodslee Avenue, Paris, Ontario.
Tel: 1800 263 2664

GHANA: Challenge Enterprises of Ghana, PO Box 5723, Accra.
Tel: (021) 222437/223249 Fax: (021) 226227

HONG KONG: Cross Communications Ltd, 1/F,
562A Nathan Road, Kowloon.
Tel: 2780 1188 Fax: 2770 6229

INDIA: Crystal Communications, 10-3-18/4/1, East Marredpally,
Secunderabad – 500 026.
Tel/Fax: (040) 7732801

KENYA: Keswick Bookshop, PO Box 10242, Nairobi.
Tel: (02) 331692/226047 Fax: (02) 728557

MALAYSIA: Salvation Book Centre (M) Sdn Bhd,
23 Jalan SS 2/64, 47300 Petaling Jaya, Selangor.
Tel: (03) 78766411/78766797 Fax: (03) 78757066/78756360

NEW ZEALAND: CMC Australasia, PO Box 36015, Lower Hutt.
Tel: 0800 449 408 Fax: 0800 449 049

NIGERIA: FBFM, Helen Baugh House,
96 St Finbarr's College Road, Akoka, Lagos.
Tel: (01) 7747429/4700218/825775/827264

PHILIPPINES: OMF Literature Inc, 776 Boni Avenue,
Mandaluyong City.
Tel: (02) 531 2183 Fax: (02) 531 1960

REPUBLIC OF IRELAND: Scripture Union, 40 Talbot Street,
Dublin 1.
Tel: (01) 8363764

SINGAPORE: Armour Publishing Pte Ltd,
Block 203A Henderson Road, 11–06 Henderson Industrial Park,
Singapore 159546.
Tel: 276 9976 Fax: 276 7564

SOUTH AFRICA: Struik Christian Books, 80 MacKenzie Street,
PO Box 1144, Cape Town 8000.
Tel: (021) 462 4360 Fax: (021) 461 3612

SRI LANKA: Christombu Books, 27 Hospital Street, Colombo 1.
Tel: (01) 433142/328909

TANZANIA: CLC Christian Book Centre, PO Box 1384,
Mkwepu Street, Dar es Salaam.
Tel/Fax (022) 2119439

USA: Cook Communications Ministries, PO Box 98, 55 Woodslee
Avenue, Paris, Ontario, Canada.
Tel: 1800 263 2664

ZIMBABWE: Word of Life Books, Shop 4, Memorial Building,
35 S Machel Avenue, Harare.
Tel: (04) 781305 Fax: (04) 774739

For email addresses, visit the CWR website: **www.cwr.org.uk**

Trusted
All Over the World

Daily Devotionals

Books and Videos

Day and Residential Courses

Counselling Training

Biblical Study Courses

Regional Seminars

Ministry to Women

CWR have been providing training and resources for Christians since the 1960s. From our headquarters at Waverley Abbey House we have been serving God's people with a vision to help apply God's Word to everyday life and relationships. The daily devotional *Every Day with Jesus* is read by over half-a-million people in more than 150 countries, and our unique courses in biblical studies and pastoral care are respected all over the world.

For a free brochure about our seminars and courses or a catalogue of CWR resources please contact us at the following address.

CWR,
Waverley Abbey House,
Waverley Lane,
Farnham,
Surrey GU9 8EP

Telephone: 01252 784700
Email: mail@cwr.org.uk
Website: www.cwr.org.uk